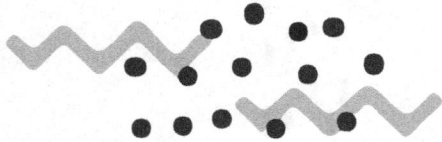

HOW TO DRAW
CUTE ANIMALS

PIXEL
studio

ISBN: 9798324496371

THIS BOOK
belongs to:

_____

LET'S START!

Look at the steps:
Before you start drawing, carefully look at all the steps and decide where you want to draw your little animal.

Draw lightly:
Start with light lines, then add stronger ones when you feel more confident.

Don't worry about mistakes:
Don't stress if something doesn't turn out perfectly. Those little mistakes make your drawing unique!

Be creative:
Add more details, take inspiration from the original drawings or come up with your own ideas to make your drawing super interesting.

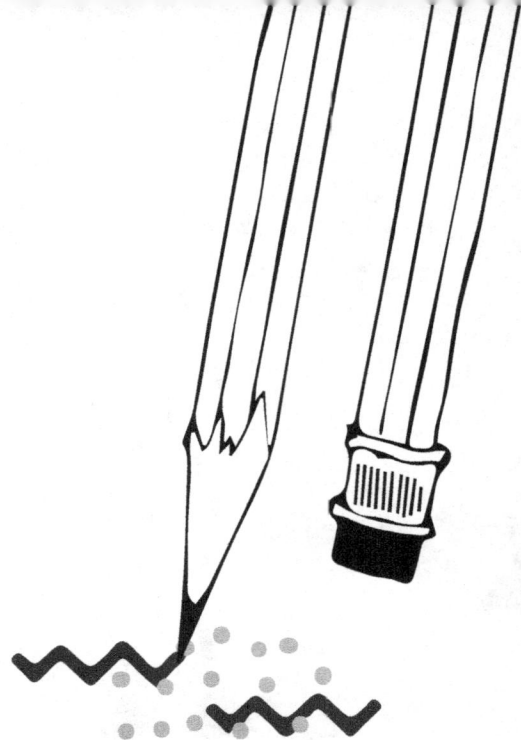

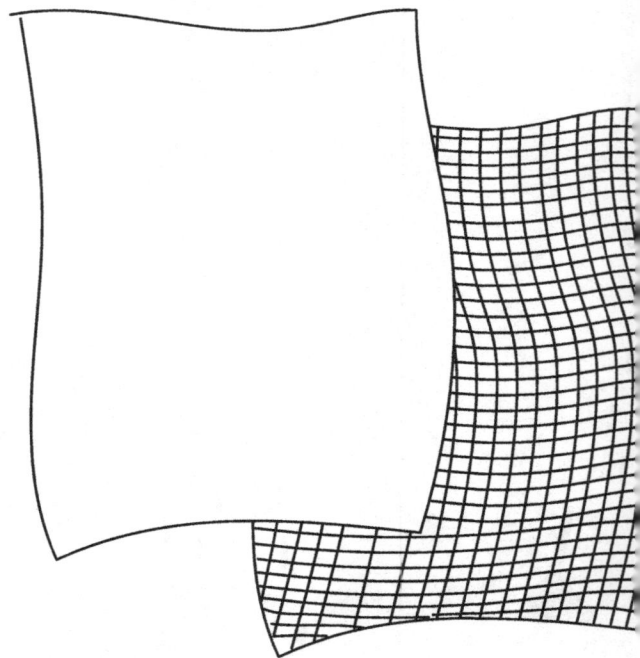

TOOLS

Prepare a sharp pencil and an eraser:
Start drawing using sharp pencils and an eraser, they allow you to make corrections and not worry when something doesn't go as planned. When you finish drawing, use colorful crayons to bring your drawings to life. Crayons are like magical wands that make your little animal look even more beautiful.

Character family:
Once you've learned drawing one character, try drawing a whole family for them, adding different sizes and details. It will be a super fun drawing adventure!

Invite to play:
Also, ask your friends or family to join you in coloring. It's a cool experience where everyone can have their own, magical world of colors!

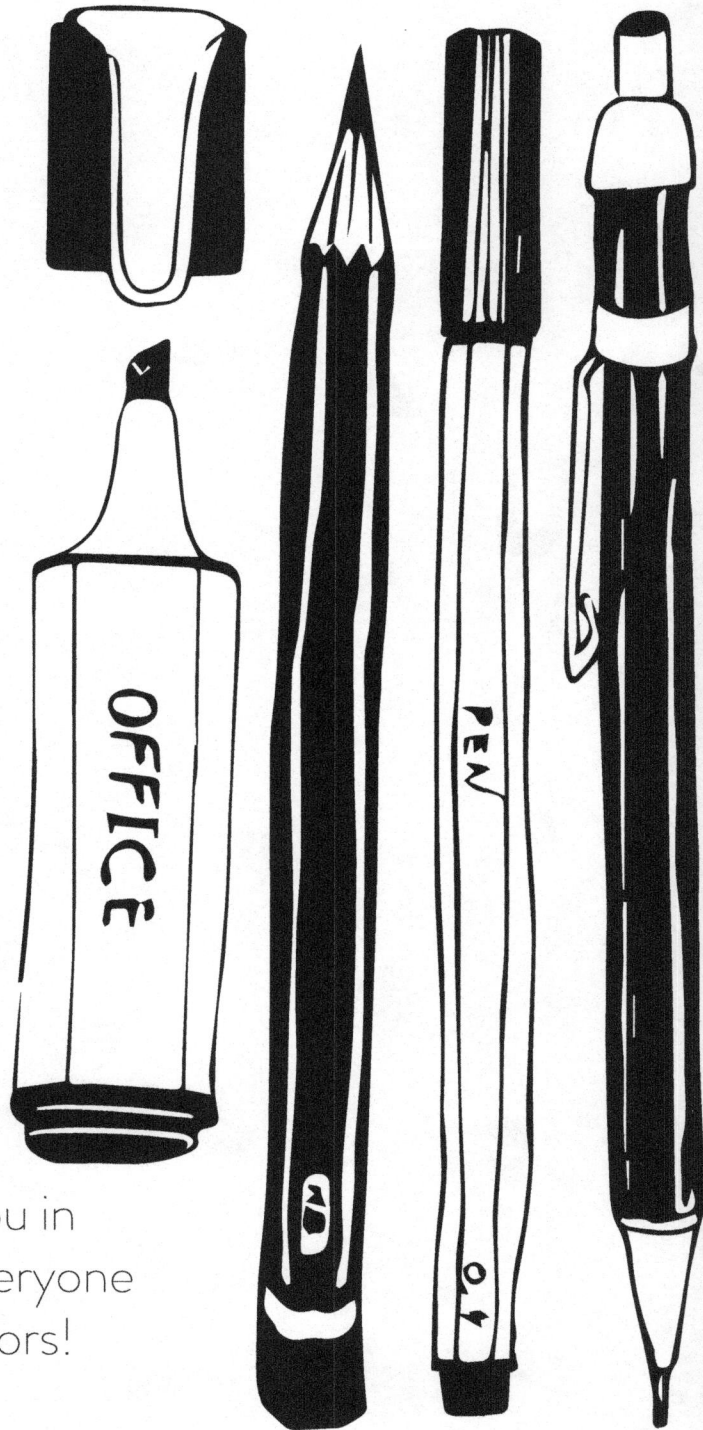

OFFICE

PEN

ANIMALS:

bat	10
bear	12
bee	14
bird	16
butterfly	18
cat	20
caterpilar	22
chicken	24
cow	26
crocodile	28
dog	30
dolphin	32
duck	34
elephant	36
fish	38
frog	40
giraffe	42
goat	44

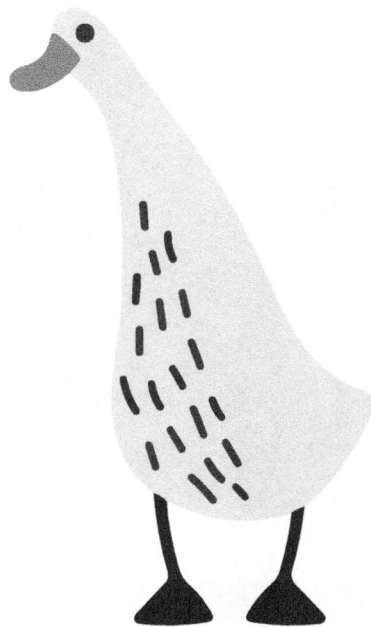

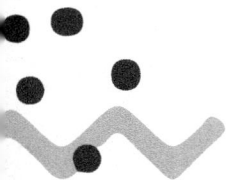

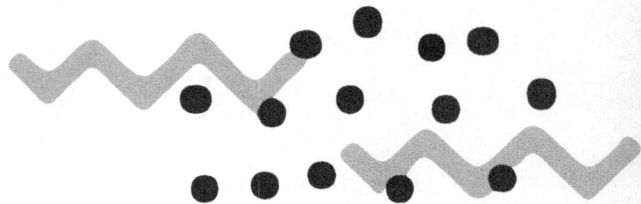

BAT

The Mexican bat is an exceptionally fast creature, capable of reaching speeds of up to 100 mph.

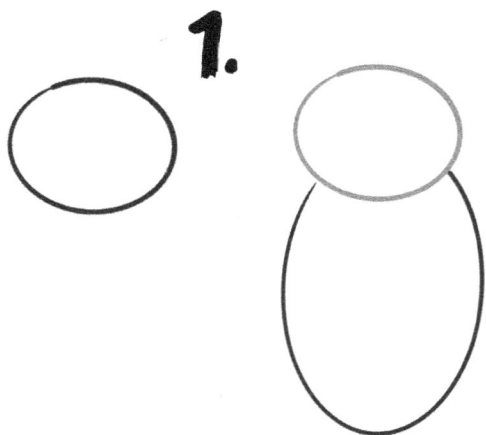

1.

Start with two round shapes forming the head and body.

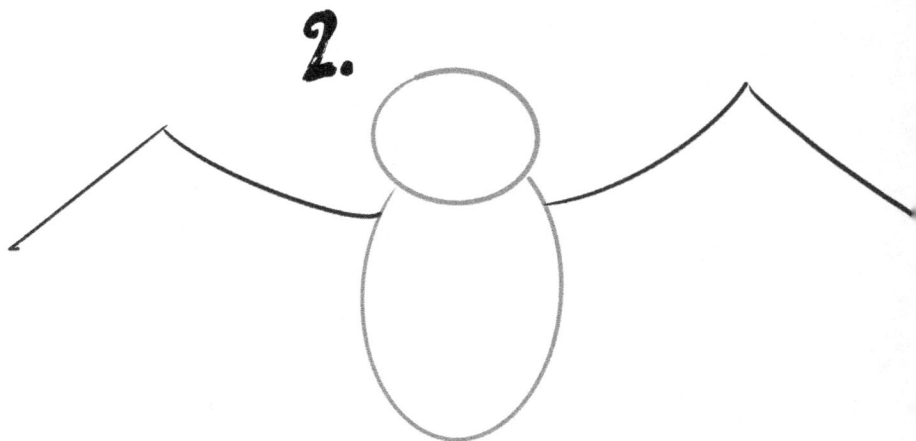

2.

Draw an arc and a straight line to create the upper part of the wings.

3.

From the point where the lines joined in the previous step, draw two curved lines.

4.

Close the wings with C-shaped lines.

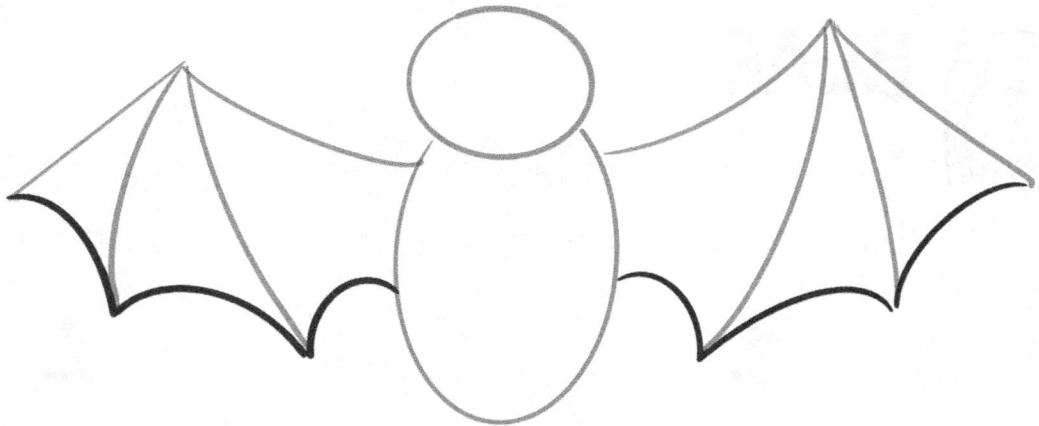

5.

Add eyes, a smile, fangs, and ears.

6.

Finish with details as you like.

11

BEAR

The American black bear is super skilled!
He can open twisty jars and doors with ease!

1.

Start with a kidney bean
shape for the body.

2.

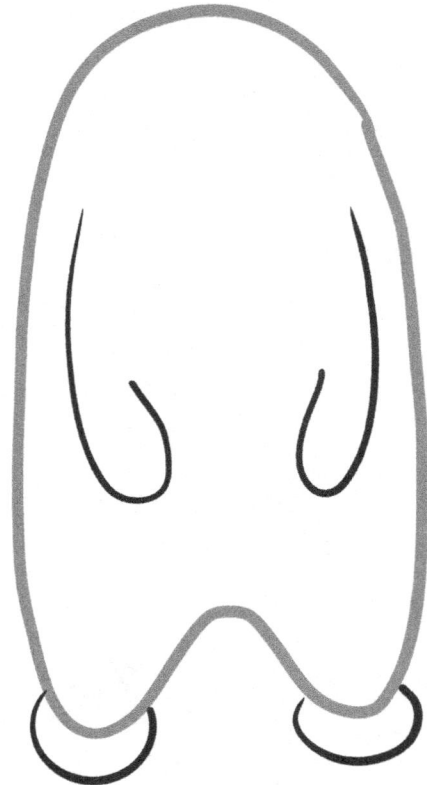

Add paws.

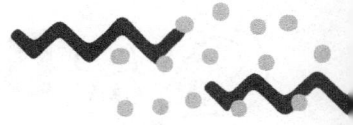

3.

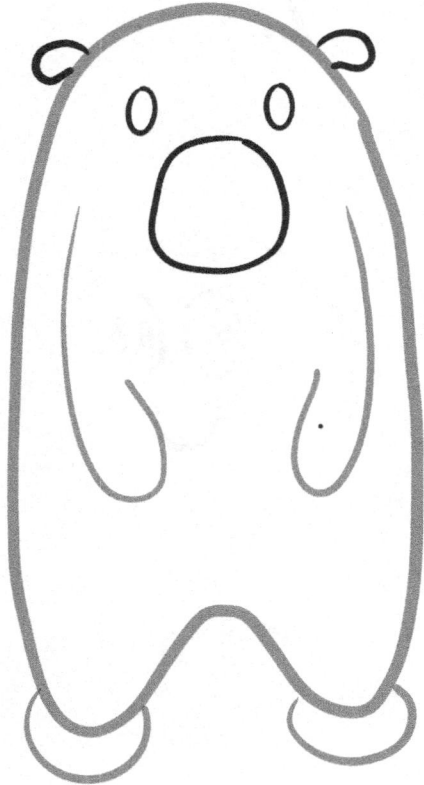

Include ears, eyes, and a round
shape that will make the snout.

4.

Draw a small nose, a smile,
and tiny claws.

BEE

The average flight range of bees is 2 miles, and the maximum can exceed 6 miles.

1.

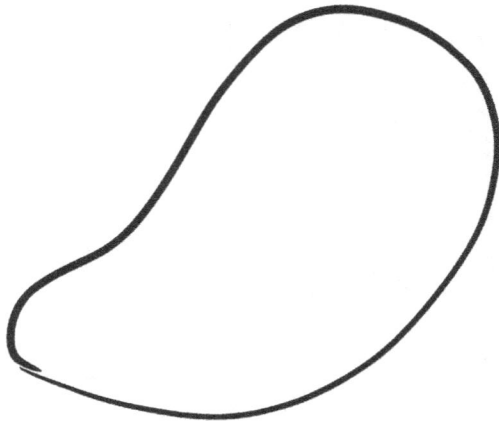

Start with a kidney bean shape for the body.

2.

Add eyes and a cute, wide smile,

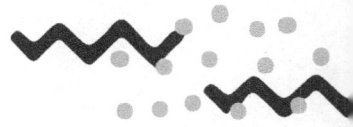

3.

4.

Antennae, little wings,
stripes, and legs.

Finish by filling in the stripes
and adding details to the wings.

BIRD

Wow, some hunting birds are speed champions!
They can dive through the air at speeds faster than 200 mph!

1.

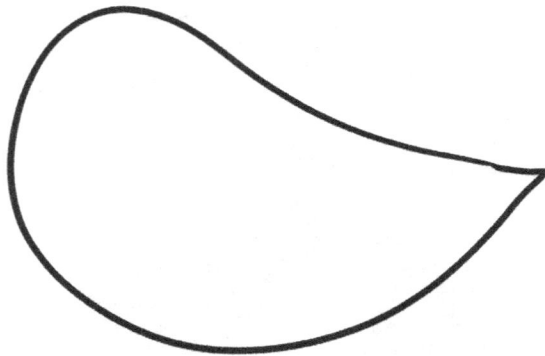

Start with a simple body shape.

2.

Add wings and a tail,
try different shapes.

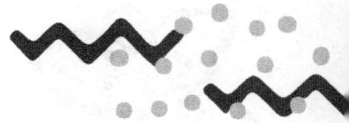

3.

Draw a beak, eyes, and tiny legs.

4.

Add a few funny details. Done!

BUTTERFLY

Although butterflies have two eyes equipped with thousands of lenses, they see only a few colors - green, yellow, and red.

1.

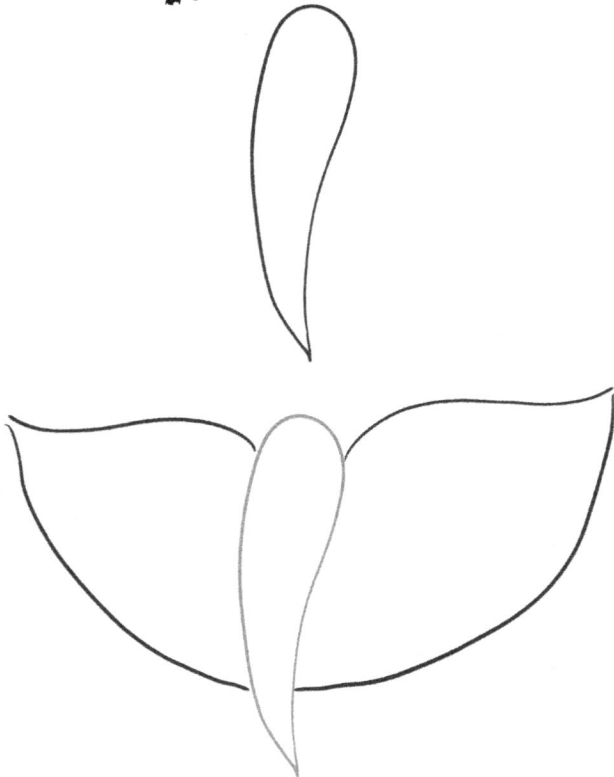

Start with a long shape for the body. Then, draw the upper part of the wings.

2.

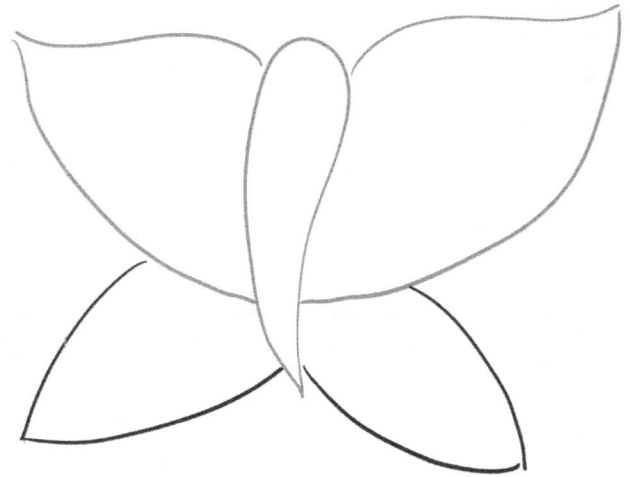

Add the lower part of the wings.

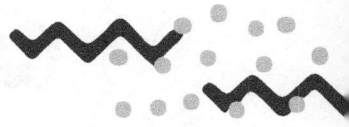

3.

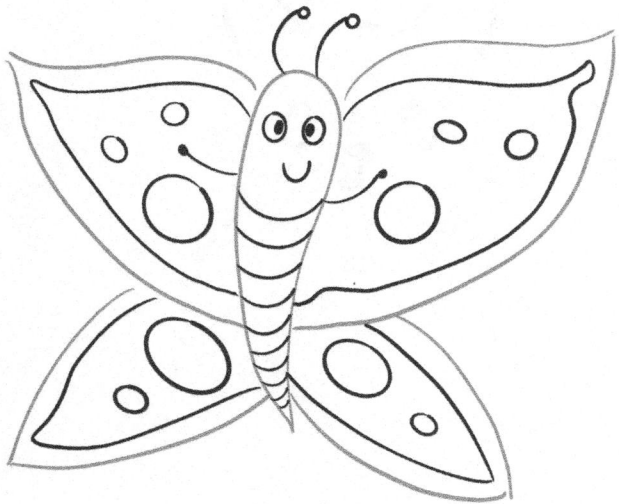

Draw antennae, eyes, and a big smile.
Try different shapes on the wings.

4.

Finish with details as you like.

CAT

Cats are famous for their napping skills! They can snooze for up to 18 hours, which is almost 70% of their lives. That's a lot of cat naps!

1.

2.

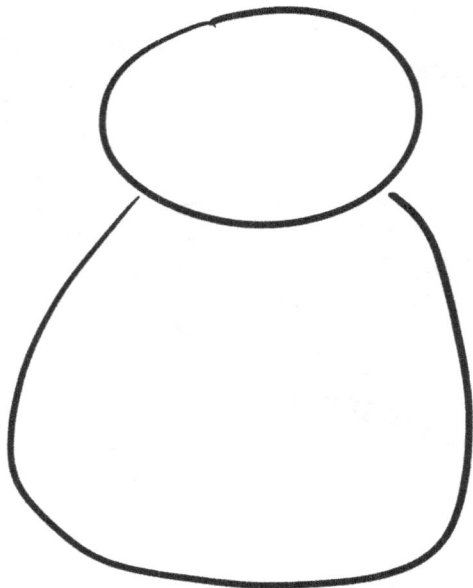

Start with two circles -
head and body.

Add pointed ears, eyes,
a nose and a nice smile.

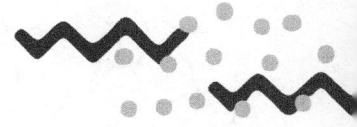

3.

Add whiskers and paws.

4.

Finish with some details, experiment
with different shapes and colors.

CATERPILLAR

Caterpillars are super hungry! In just a few weeks, their big job is to eat a lot – like 27,000 times their own weight! They are like eating champions!

1.

Start with a round circle; that will be the head.

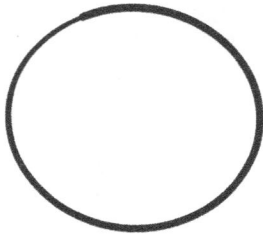

2.

Now, add more circles to make the entire caterpillar body.

3.

Draw antennae, eyes, and a big smile.

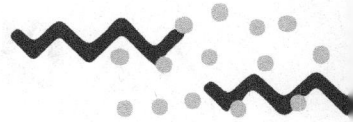

4.

Add lots of little legs!

5.

Finish by adding all the
cool details you like!

CHICKEN

Chickens can sleep on one leg. When they feel safe and relaxed, they can lift one leg and take a nap on the other! Isn't that amazing? This way, they can rest while standing on one leg, ready to run away if something surprises them. Chickens are real balancing experts!

1.

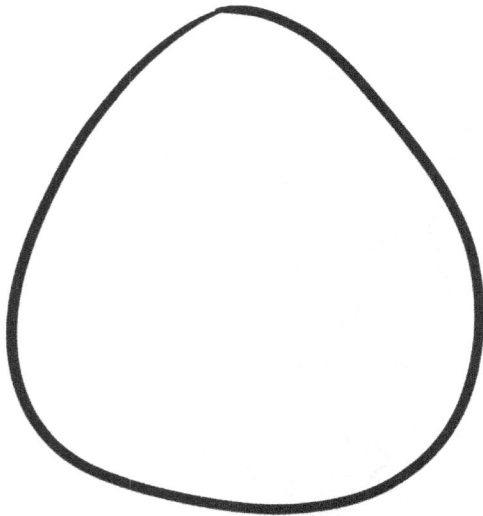

Start with a round body shape.

2.

Add a crest and tail,

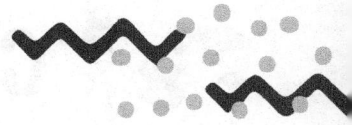

3.

Eyes, beak,

4.

Wings and legs.

25

 # COW

Cows have best friends, just like people do! If their favorite pals aren't around, cows can feel a bit sad. They like hanging out with their best buddies!

 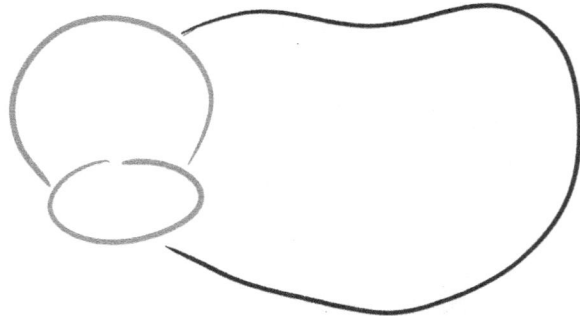

Start with two round shapes forming the head

Then, add a bean-like shape for the body.

Add horns and ears,

Legs and tail.

4.

Eyes and udder,

5.

Spots.

6.

Finally, fill in the spots.

CROCODILE

An adult crocodile can survive without eating for up to a year. This is possible due to a slow metabolism and low energy requirements.

1.

Start with a round nose, then draw a line
for the body all the way to the tip of the tail.

2.

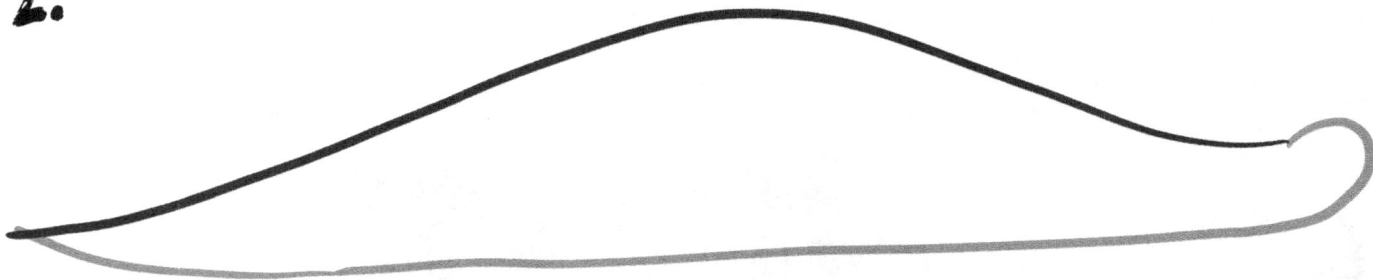

Close the body shape with an arched back.

3.

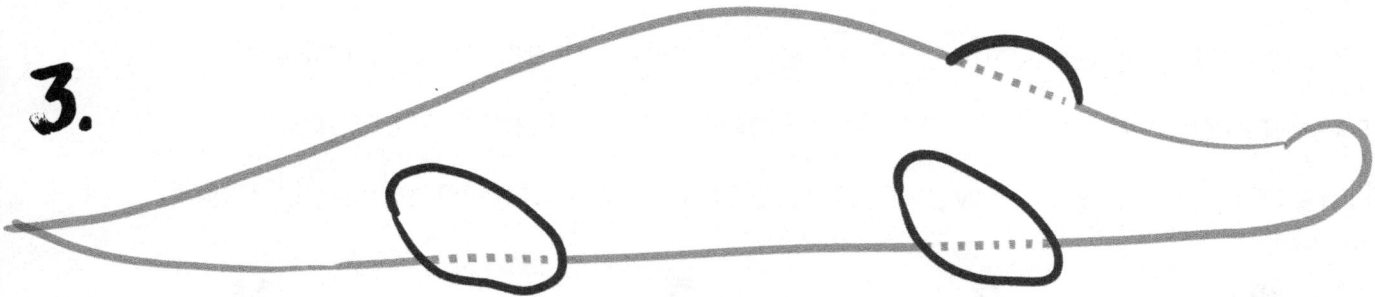

Add legs and a spot for the eye.

4.

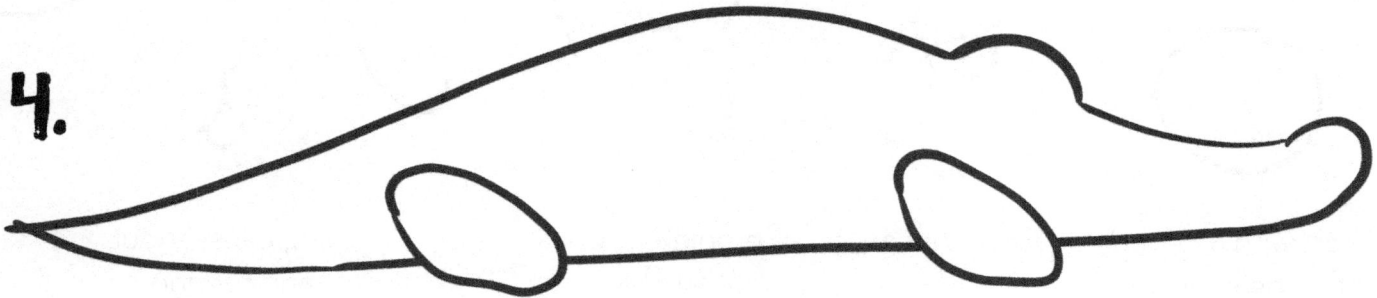

Remove unnecessary lines segments.

5.

Add an eye, a sly smile, big teeth and claws,
and details as desired. Done!

 # DOG

Dogs are super sniffers! Their sense of smell is amazing, it is up to 100,000 times more powerful than ours. This makes them awesome at tracking and finding things.

1.

Start with a circle for the snout.

2.

Add a nose.

3.

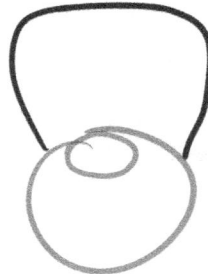

Complete the rest of the head.

4.

Ears, eyes, snout, and tongue.

5.

Draw a backline, a front paw, and a back paw.

6.

Complete the back paw.

7. Add the belly and the remaining paws...

8. ... and a wagging tail –
the essential for every dog!

1.

2.

3.

Every dog is unique! Try playing around
with different shapes for snouts and ears!

DOLPHIN

Dolphins are amazing! They actually give names to their babies. Scientists found special sounds in their language, that only certain dolphins respond to.

1.

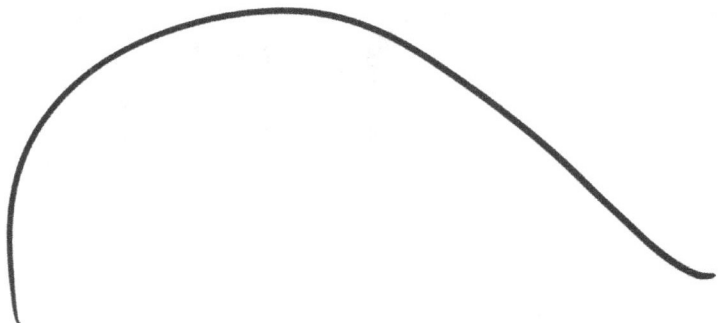

Start with the shape of the back.

2.

Add a C-shape nose.

3.

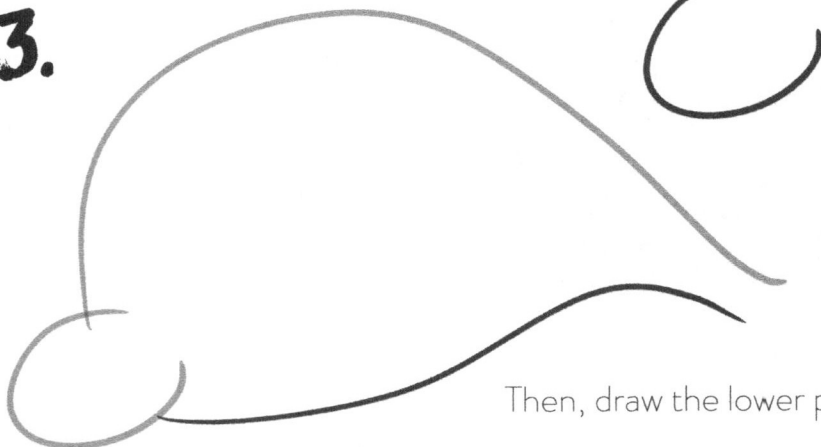

Then, draw the lower part of the body.

4.

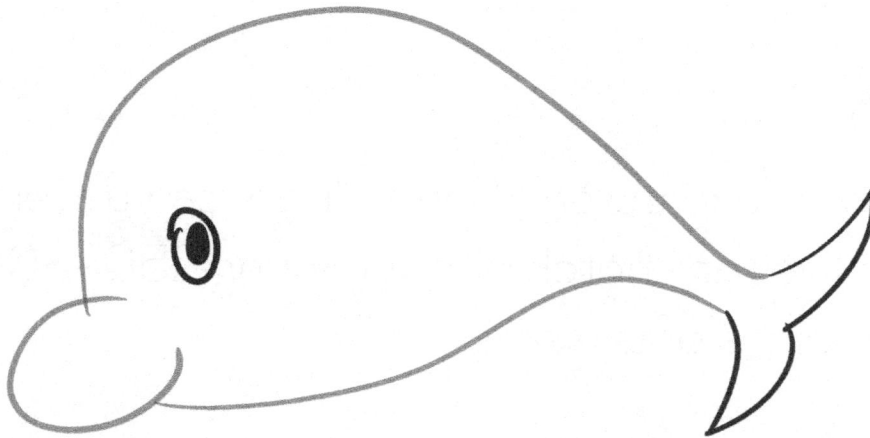

Add a cute eye and tail.

5.

Draw the fins.

6.

Finish with details as you like.
You can add air bubbles
because dolphins spend most
of their time underwater!

DUCK

Ducks are like little adventurers! Some ducks can travel really far in a day, with the top-notch ones covering 250-300 miles. They're the champions of the sky!

1.

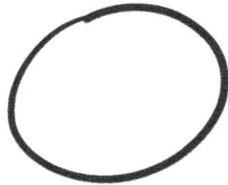

Start with a circle for the head.

2.

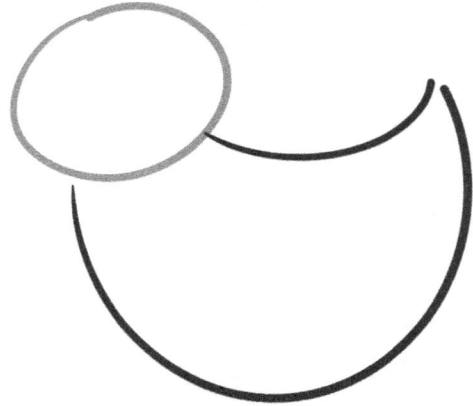

Then draw the shape of the body.

3.

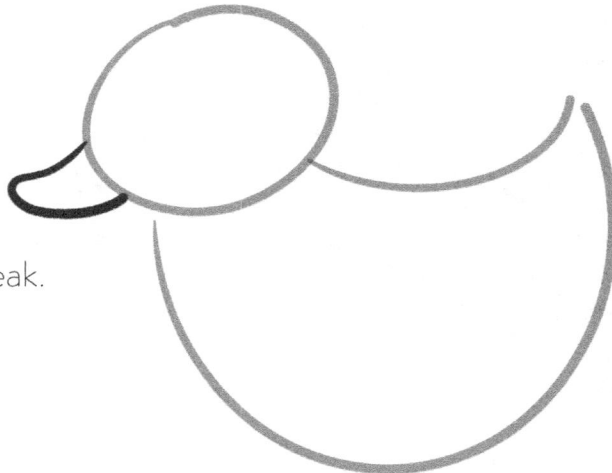

Add a little beak.

4.

Eye, wing, and tail.

5.

A little tuft on the head.

Ducks can swim and walk, so you can draw legs or place the duck on water.

6.

ELEPHANT

Elephants are big food lovers! They spend as much as 16 hours a day munching on tasty treats. Also, did you know elephants are the only mammals that can't jump? They're unique!

1.

2.

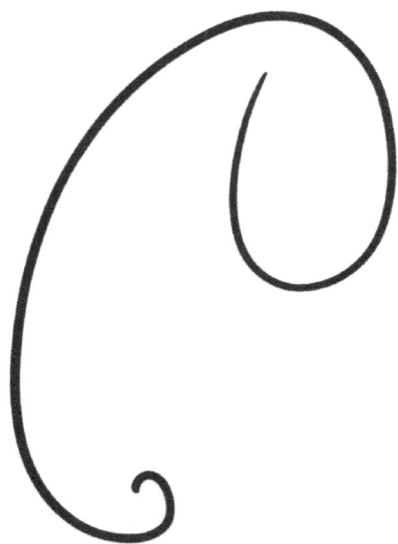

Begin by drawing a curled shape - that will be the ear and trunk.

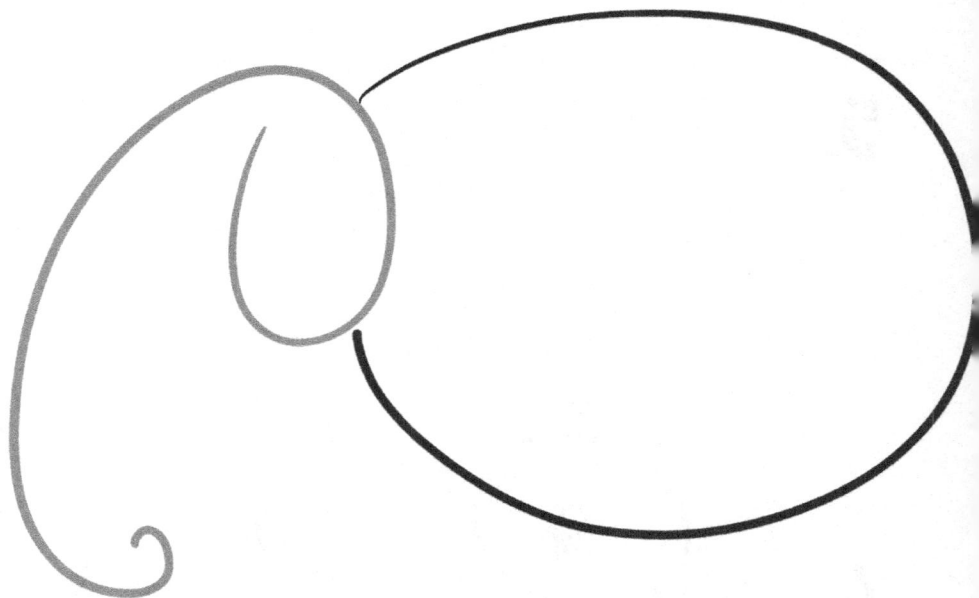

Draw a rounded body shape.

3.

Add tusks and
four sturdy legs.

4.

Include a tail,
finish the trunk,
and add small
details like toes.

FISH

Did you know that some fish are super-speedy?
The fastest fish can swim as fast as 50 mph!

1.

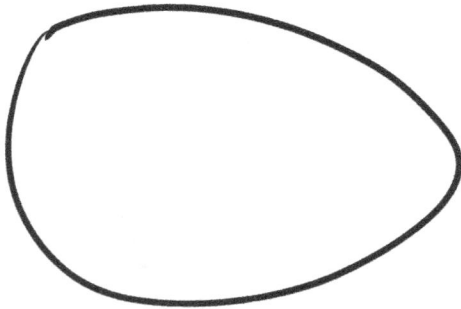

Draw a round shape for the fish's body.
Fish come in all sorts - experiment
with different shapes - long, short,
thin, chubby.

2.

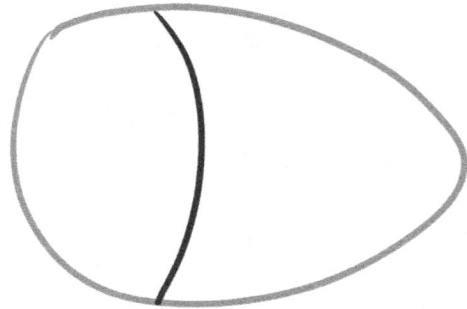

Add a line to separate the head
from the rest of the body.

3.

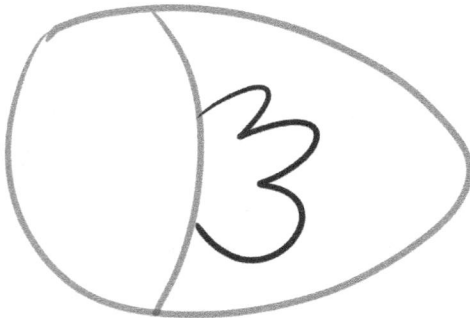

Draw the side fin.

4.

Add other fins and the tail.

5.

Next, add an eye
and a little mouth.

6.

Add some lines
on the fins and tail.

7.

Add scales.

FROG

One species of frog – the glass frog is like a little magical creature! It's super tiny, only 1 inch long, and it has see – through skin and muscles, which make its internal organs clearly visible.

1.

Start with three semicircles
– those will be the eyes and
the forehead.

2.

Add a big round shape that
will be the frog's body.

3.

Then, draw froggy thighs,

4.

Little froggy feet,

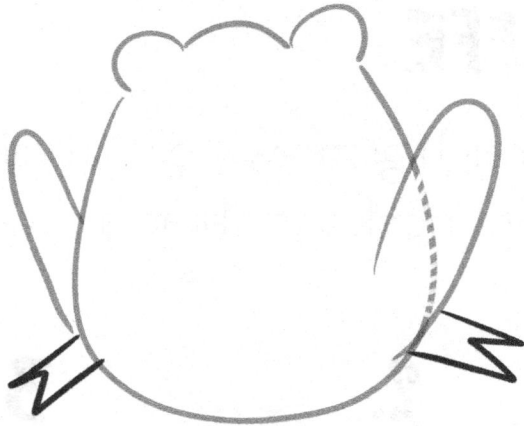

5.

Froggy arms,

6.

Finally, add small froggy
eyes and a wide smile!

GIRAFFE

Even though giraffes are incredibly tall, they have the same number of neck vertebrae as humans, which is seven.

1.

2.

3.

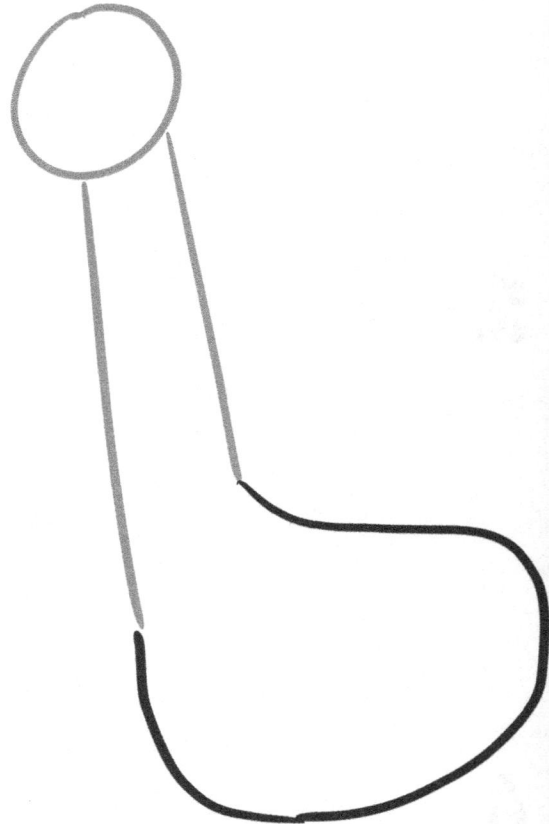

Start with a circle - that will be the giraffe's head.

Then, draw the neck.

Add the body of the giraffe.

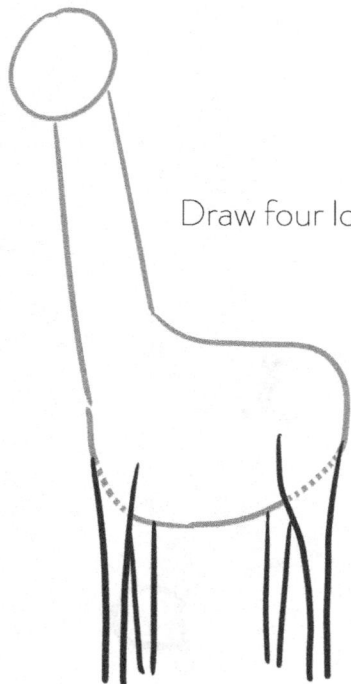

4. Draw four long legs.

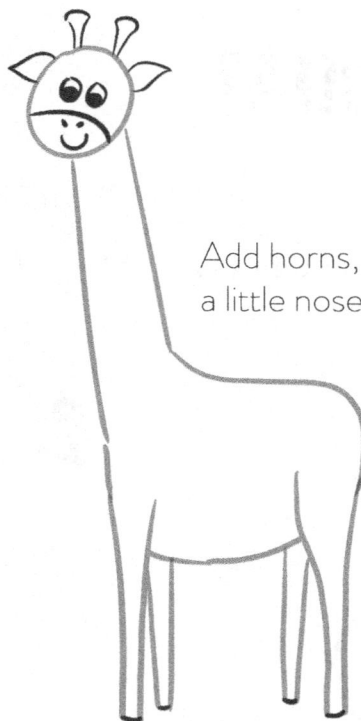

5. Add horns, ears, eyes, a little nose, and a smile.

6. Mark spots all over the giraffe's body.

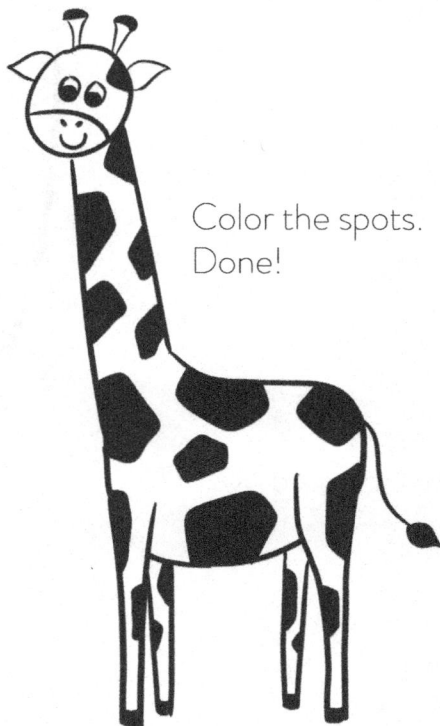

7. Color the spots. Done!

 # GOAT

Goats were the very first animals humans took care of, over 9,000 years ago!

1.

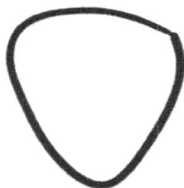

2.

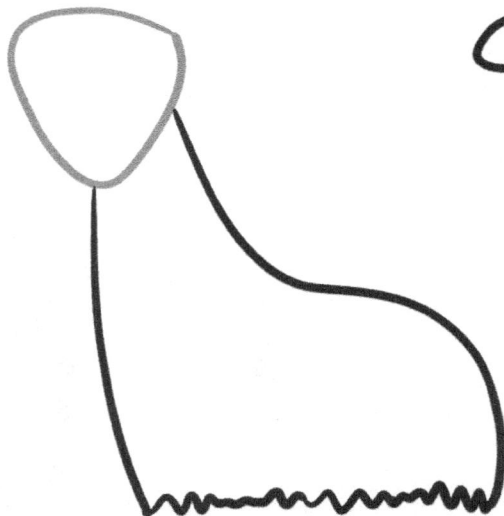

3.

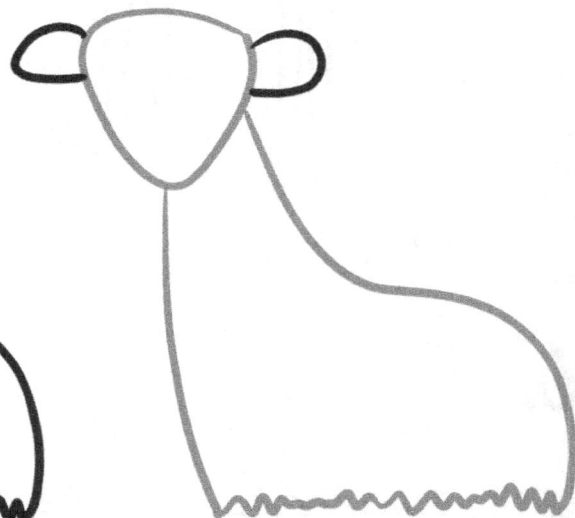

Start with a pointed oval.

Then, draw the body.

Now, add ears.

4.

Next, give her a tousled goat beard, a tail, and four little legs.

5.

Just horns left.

6.

Finally, add some cool details. Done!

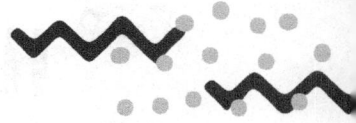

45

HAMSTER

Hamsters have special cheek pouches; these "pockets" can hold food weighing up to half their body weight.

1.

2.

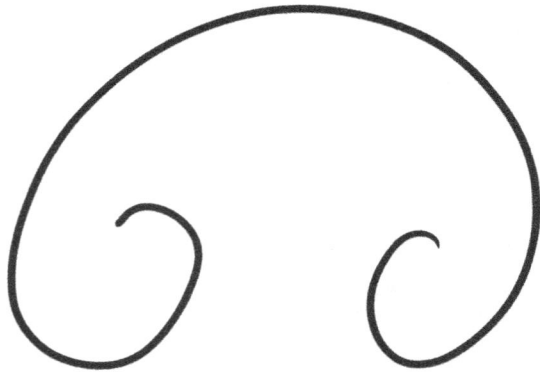

Start with a swirl to create
the forehead and cheeks.

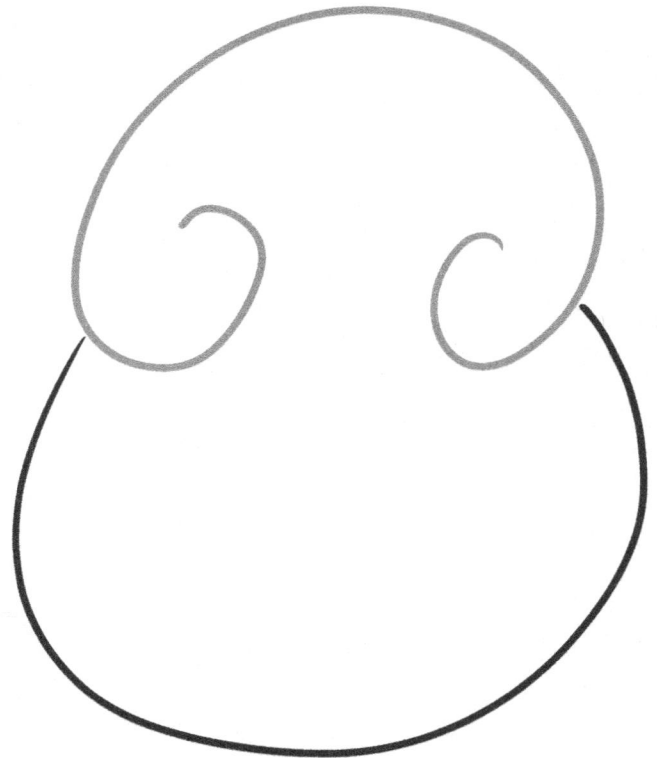

Then, draw the rest
of the body.

3.

Add little ears, eyes,
nose, and a mouth.

4.

Finally, add four tiny paws
and finish with details as you like.

HEDGEHOG

On a hedgehog's back, there can be from 5,000 to 7,000 spines! They're like tiny armor that keeps them safe.

1.

2.

Start with a pointy snout and a round nose. Then, add a wide smile, an eye, and a little ear.

Draw spikes that will be the body of the hedgehog.

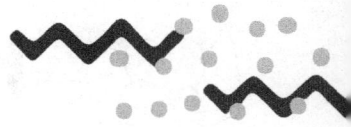

3.

Add spikes separating the
head from the rest of the
body and the paws.

4.

More spikes! Done!

HIPPO

Hippos can sweat red, producing a special red fluid that keeps their skin healthy!

1.

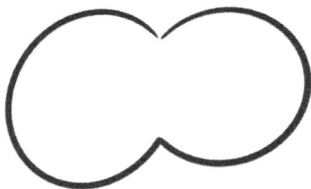

Start with a shape resembling an horizontal eight - that will be the snout.

2.

Add a heart - shaped figure, that will be the rest of the head.

3.

Draw eyes, nostrils, ears, and a little snout.

4.

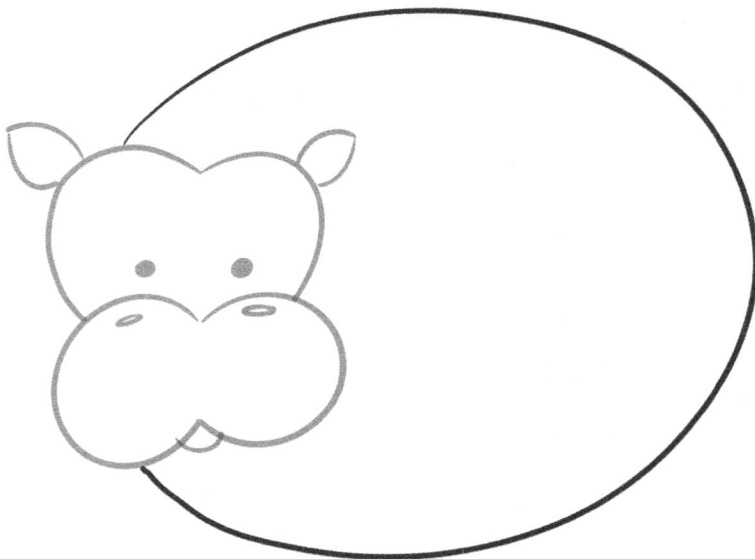

Sketch a large oval, which will be the hippo's body.

5.

Add thick, short legs and a tail

6.

Finish with details.

 # HORSE

Horses use their ears, eyes, and noses to show how they feel, just like how we use our faces to show if we're happy or sad!

1.

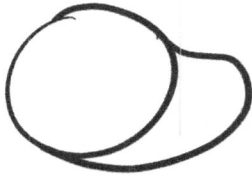

Construct the horse's head
using round shapes.

2.

Draw the torso in
the shape of a bean.

3.

Add four legs.

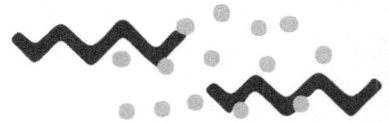

4.

Draw ears, nostrils, a smile, and hooves.

5.

Now it's time for a thick mane and tail! Erase any unnecessary lines.

6.

Finish with details.

KANGAROO

Kangaroos are super jumpers! They can leap as far as 10 feet and go as fast as a car!

1.

Start with a circle for the head.

2.

Then, add long ears.

3.

Draw an oval shape for the body.

4.

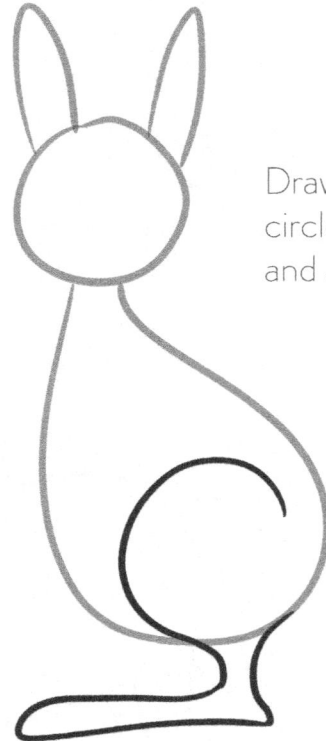

Draw an incomplete circle for the thigh and a long paw.

5.

Add a tail and
the other paw.

6.

Now, draw smaller front
paws and a pouch.

7.

Draw the eyes
and muzzle.

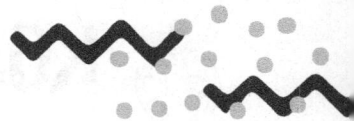

KOALA

Baby koalas ride in a special pouch on their mom's belly, just like baby kangaroos. It's cool how both animals use pouches to take care of their babies!

1.

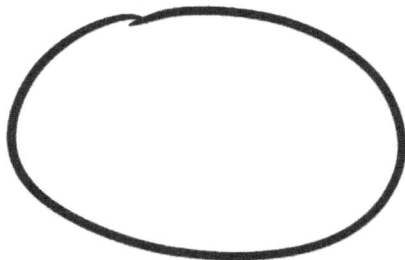

Start with a flattened circle - that will be the head.

2.

Add a large, characteristic nose, eyes, and a smile.

3.

Draw big round ears.

4.

Sketch an oval for the koala's body.

5.

Finally, add paws and a tummy.

 # LADYBUG

Ladybugs in their lifetime can eat about 5000 aphids.

1.

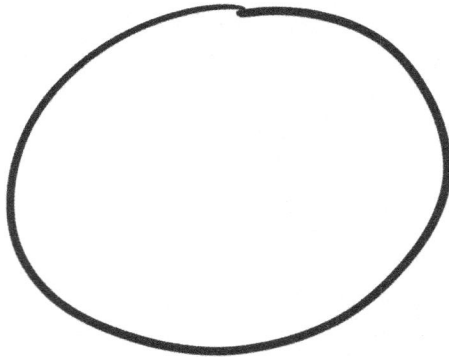

Start with an oval, which will be the body of the ladybug.

2.

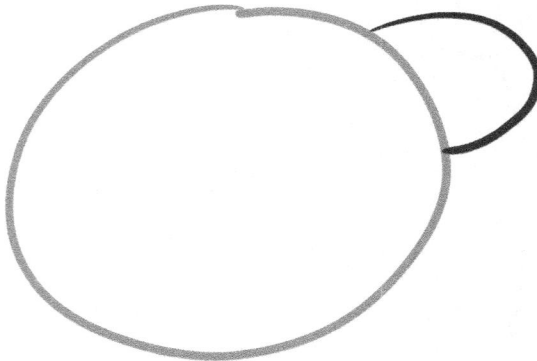

Add the head.

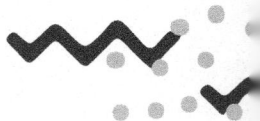

3.

Divide the body into two wings with an arched line. Draw eyes and legs.

4.

Draw antennae and dots.

5.

Finish with details, color the dots black.

LION

Lions can roar so loud that you can hear them from 4 miles away! But when people shout to each other, our voices can only be heard from up to 1,000 feet away.

1.

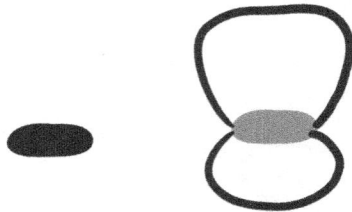

Draw a round, flattened nose. Then, at the top and bottom of the nose, add two rounded shapes that will make the head.

2.

Add ears, eyes, and a smile.

3.

Create the mane with circular lines.

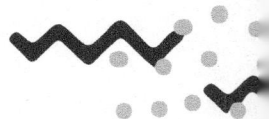

4.

Draw the lion's body with the front paw.
Experiment freely with shapes.

5.

Add the hind
leg and tail.

6.

Finished!

LLAMA

Alpacas and llamas are known to spit when they get upset.

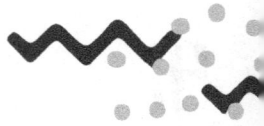

1.

To draw a llama, use a line made up of smaller semicircles. It's like drawing little clouds! Start from the top of the head.

2.

3.

4.

Add eyes, a muzzle, and horns

5.

Draw the rest of the body and the tail.

6.

Use small semicircles to outline the hooves.

7.

Now draw the legs, connecting the torso to the hooves. Add a belly.

8.

Draw the hooves and more semicircular lines. Finished!

MEERKAT

Meerkats can gobble up scorpions without getting hurt, which makes them super brave when hunting those prickly critters!

1.

2.

3.

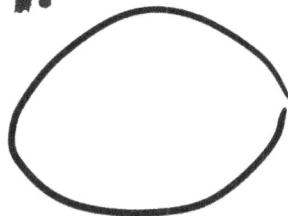

Start with a flattened, round shape - that will be the head.

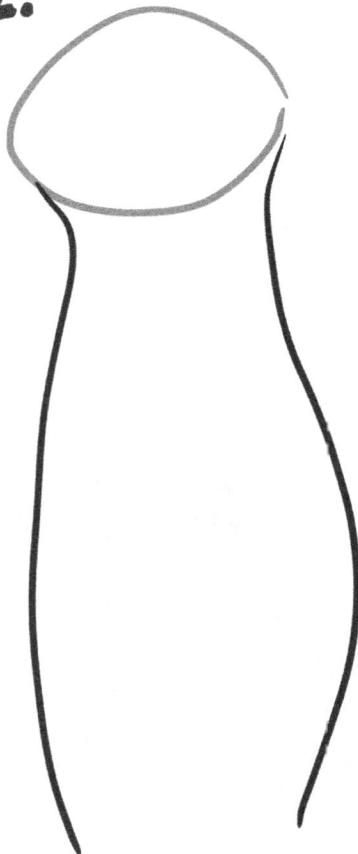

Draw two rounded lines that will create the long body of the meerkat.

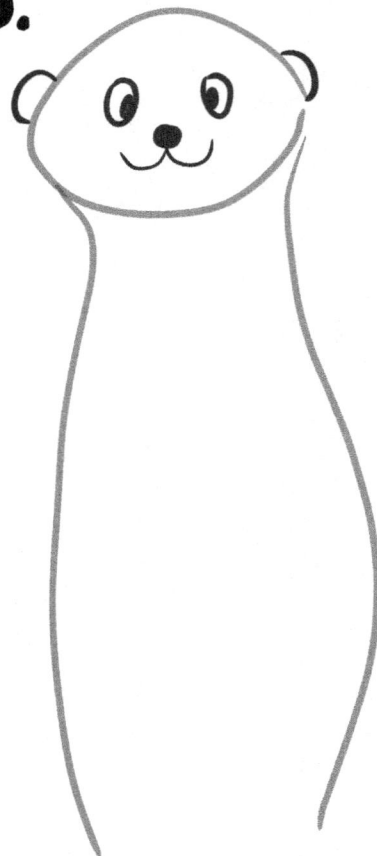

Add ears, eyes, a nose, and a smile.

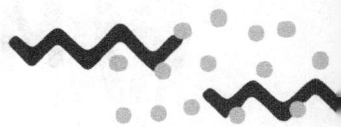

4.

Next, draw the
paws and tail.

5.

Finish with details like black
outlines around the eyes
and black stripes. Done!

65

 # MONKEY

Monkeys live in big families, kind of like ours. They can have anywhere from 6 to 10 members in their family, and sometimes they even make huge communities with up to 100 monkeys!

1.

2.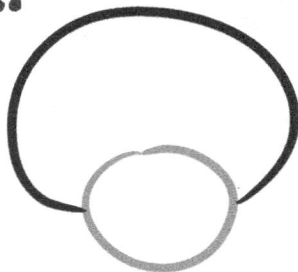

3.

4.

5.

Start with the head. A smaller circle will be the monkey's muzzle. A larger circle is for the rest of the head. Then, draw a shape like half of a heart above the muzzle; this will be the monkey's face. Now, add ears, nostrils, and a wide, monkey smile. We have a monkey's head ready!

Next, add monkey's arms and legs.

6.

Add a spiral, which will be the tail, and a curve between the arms that will enclose the monkey's body.

7.

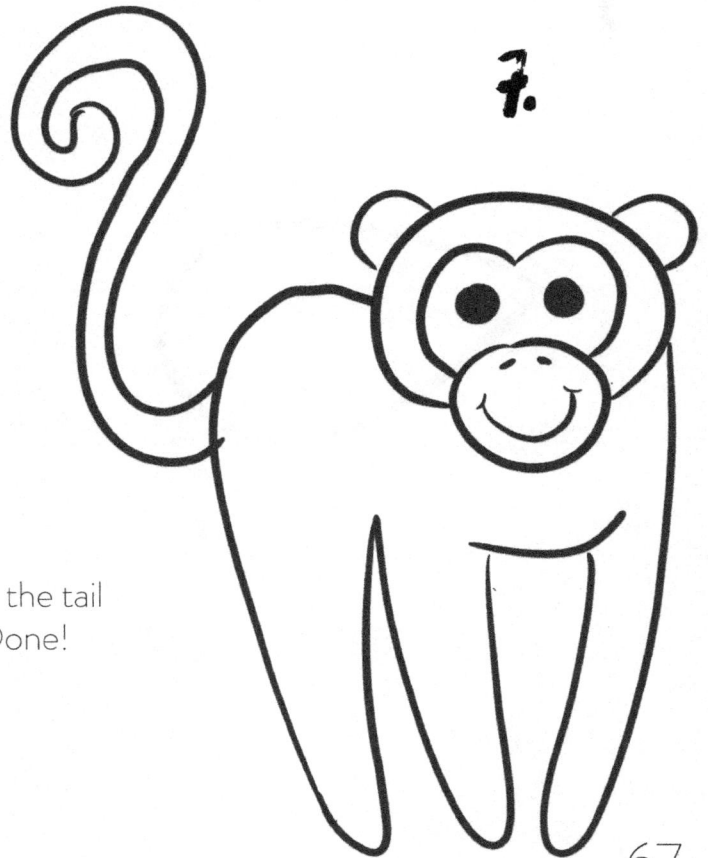

Finally, draw a second line along the tail line, which will thicken the tail. Done!

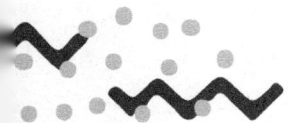

MOUSE

The Pakarana is considered to be the largest mouse in the world. It inhabits the regions of South America, and the total length of an adult individual's body can reach up to 32 inches!

1.

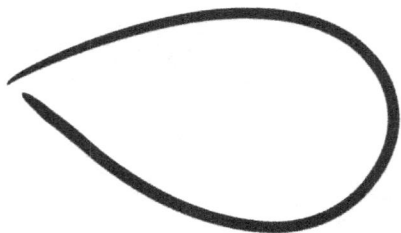

Start with a pointy shape -
that's the head.

2.

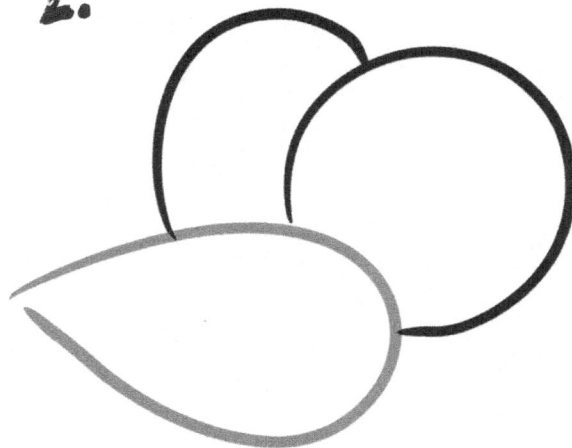

Draw big, round ears.

3.

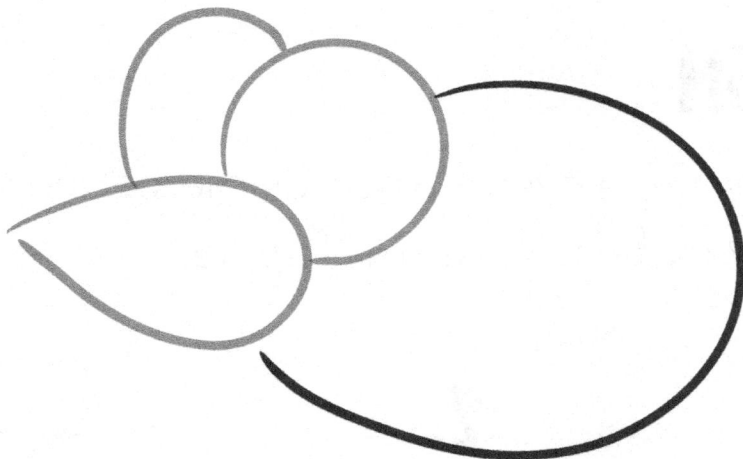

Add a round body
for the mouse.

4.

Draw little paws and
a tiny round nose.

5.

Finally, give it a smile,
an eye, and a long tail.

69

OSTRICH

Ostriches have huge eyes – their diameter can be as wide as 2 inches, like a small apple!

1.

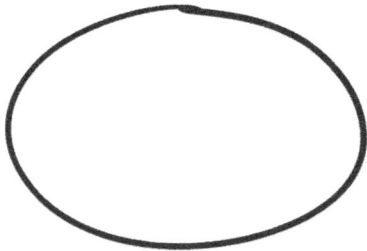

Start with an oval for the body of the ostrich.

2.

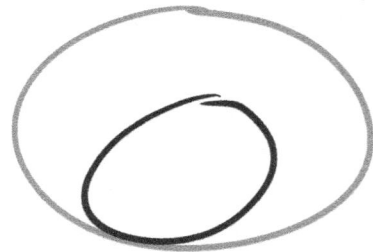

Then, draw another one inside – that will be the wing.

3.

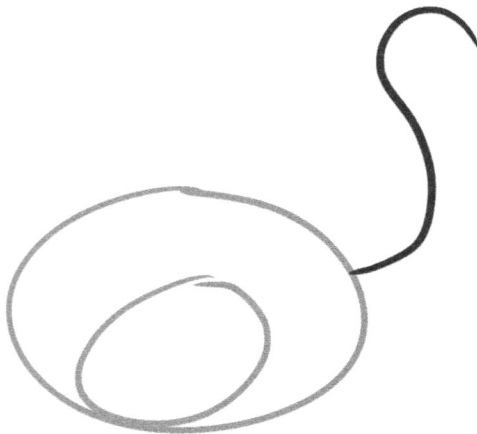

Next, sketch a line in the shape of the letter "S" for the neck and head.

4.

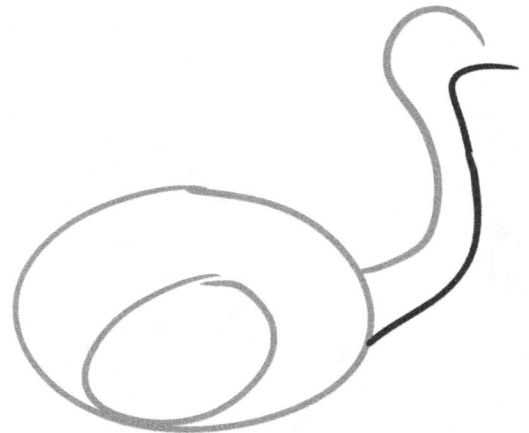

Draw another line to enclose the shape of the neck.

5.

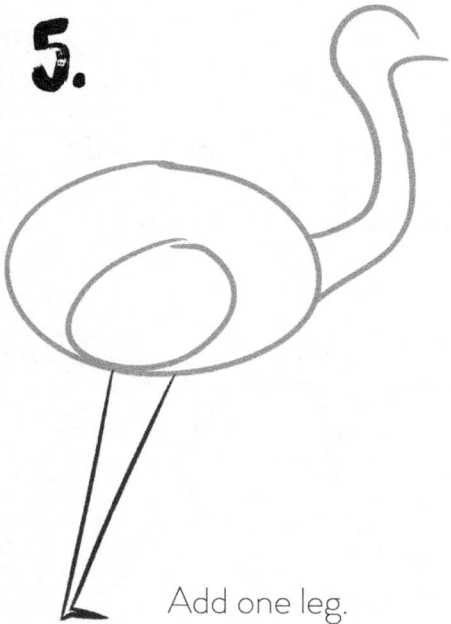

Add one leg.

6.

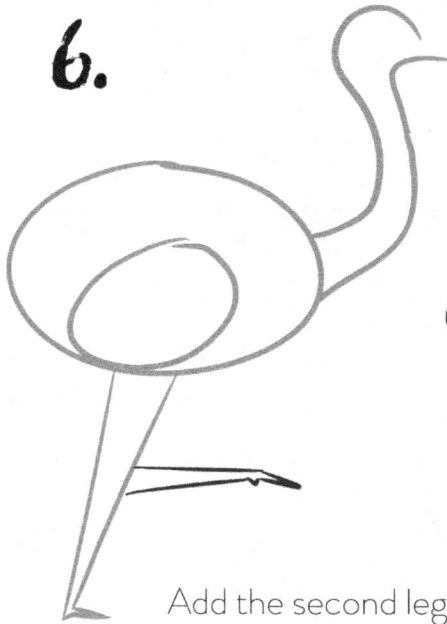

Add the second leg.

7.

Use arcs to create the wing and tail.

8.

Add the beak and eye.

9.

Finish with details – you can add feathers, adjust the tail and wing lines. Be creative!

71

OWL

The eyes of an owl work in a very useful way - they can enlarge the seen image almost like a telephoto lens.

1.

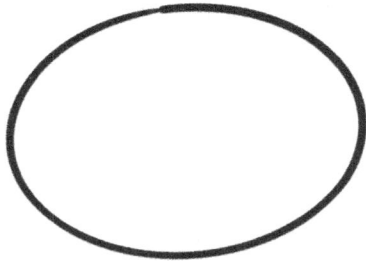

Start with a flattened circle.

2.

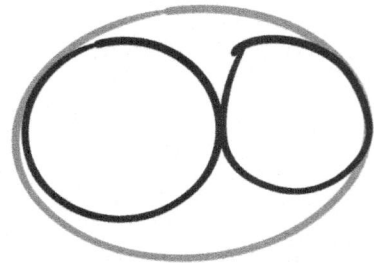

Then, inside it, add two more circles.

3.

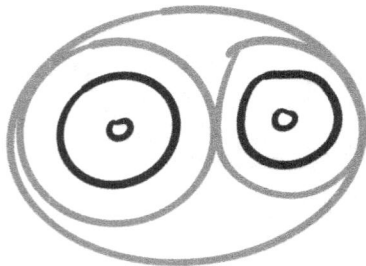

Inside, add two more circles - those will be the eyes!

4.

Draw pointy ears and a beak.

5. Add a rounded shape for the owl's body.

6. Next, draw wings by adding lines going down from the head. Use a long arc to draw the central tail feather at the bottom.

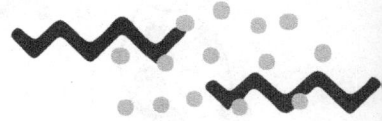

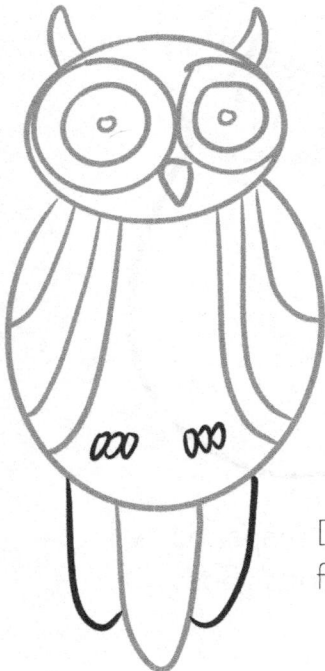

7. Draw side tail feathers and legs.

8. Finally, with gentle arcs, mark feathers on the belly. You can add a branch for the owl to perch on.

PANDA

Did you know that a panda has as many as 6 fingers?

1.

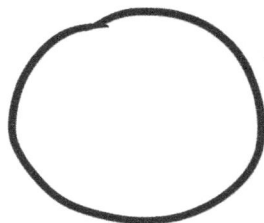

Start with a circle - that
will be the head.

2.

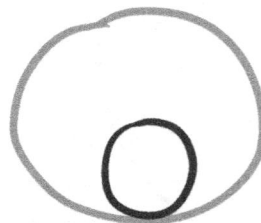

Draw another circle inside.

3.

Inside this second circle, draw
the nose and mouth. Above,
add eyes with characteristic
outlines and small ears.

4.

Draw an oval shape that will
be the panda's body.

5.

Add four paws.

6.

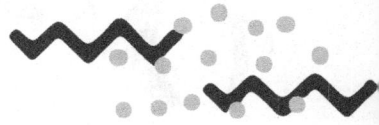

Finally, color the paws, eyes outlines, and ears black. Done!

PENGUIN

Some penguins can dive to depths of up to 1,600 feet and stay underwater for up to half an hour.

1.

Start with a semicircle - that will be the head.

2.

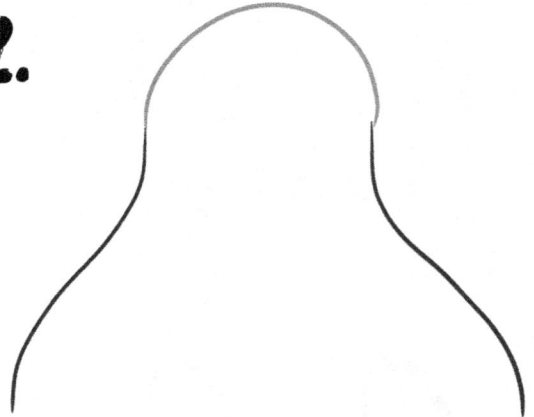

Then, from the head, draw two curved lines - those will be the wings.

3.

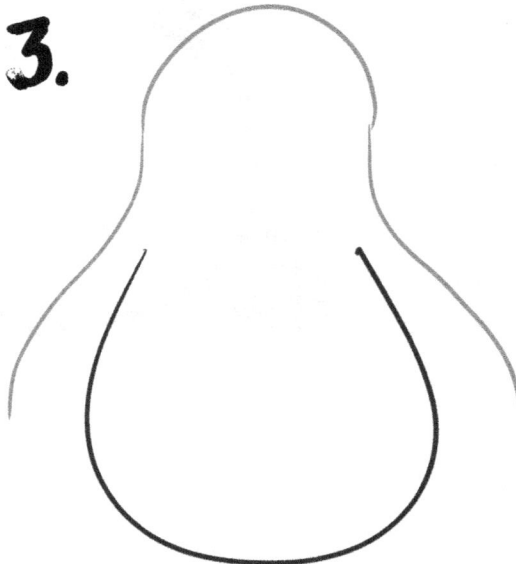

Next, add a round belly.

4.

Next, connect the belly line to the wings using gentle curves. Add eyes and a beak.

5.

Add a curved line on each wing to separate the outer part from the inner part. Draw two semicircles around the eyes, starting from the nose.

6.

Draw the flippers and add subtle curved lines to separate the light belly from the darker body.

7.

Color the penguin, distinguishing the light belly from the darker back. Done!

PIG

Mud wallowing isn't just fun for pigs, it's also an effective way to cool down their bodies.

1.

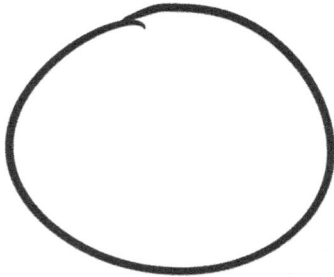

Start with a circle
for the head.

2.

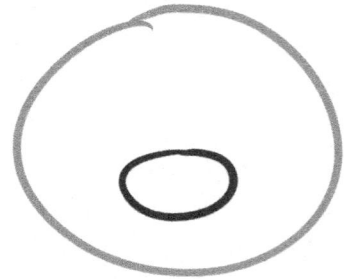

Inside the circle,
draw another circle
for the nose.

3.

Add piggy ears –
experiment with different
shapes and positions.

4. Draw a large round shape for the body.

5. Add four legs to the body, each ending with a small notch for the hooves. On the head, draw eyes, nostrils, and a smile. Erase any unnecessary lines.

6. Finally, add a curly tail. You can color the hooves a different shade and add details like mud spots as you like.

RABBIT

Rabbits have the ability of panoramic vision, meaning they can see in a range of 360 degrees. They can see all around them, like having eyes in the back of their heads!

1.

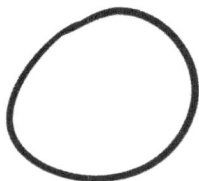

Start with a circle for the head.

2.

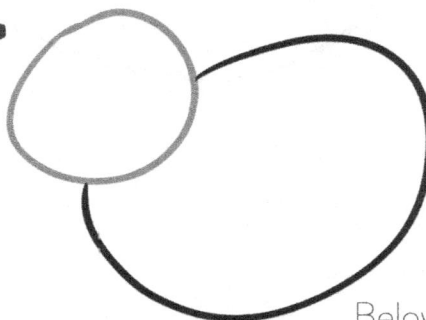

Below the head, draw another circle – that's the rabbit's body.

3.

Now, add long ears!

4.

Next, draw an eye, a nose, whiskers, and a smile.

5.

Draw two small front paws, and at the back of the rabbit, something like the letter "E" – that's the hind leg.

6.

Fluffy tail and some details like the inner ear, a tie under the chin, and little claws.

7.

Done!

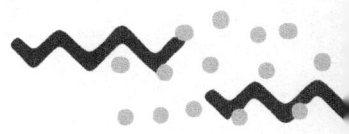

81

 # RACCOON

Raccoons have very nimble front paws, which they can use to manipulate objects, much like how humans use their hands!

1.

2.

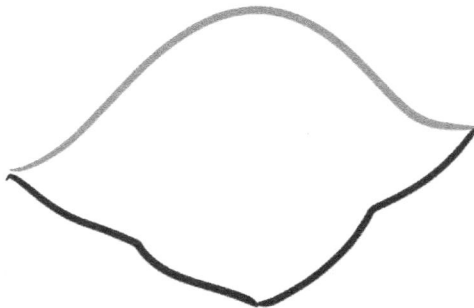

Start with a pointed shape for the head, tapering to the sides.

3.

Draw an oval shape for the body.

82

4.

Add ears, eyes, a round
snout, nose and smile.

5.

Now, draw outlines around
the eyes, just as tapered as
the head. Add paws and tail.

6.

Color the outlines black, add stripes
on the tail, a stripe on the forehead,
and draw two triangles inside the ears.

7.

Color as needed. Done!

RHINO

Rhinoceros horns continue to grow throughout their lives.
If a horn breaks or is damaged, another one grows in its place.
It's similar to human nails.

1.

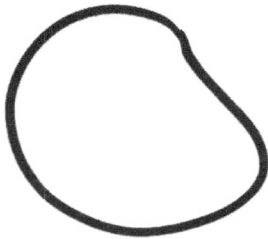

Start with a gently indented
circle, shaped similar to
a kidney - this will be the head.

2.

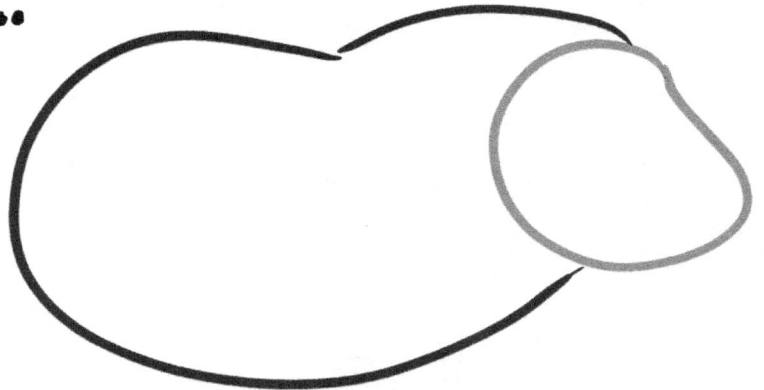

Next, draw an oval underneath, indented from the
top - that's where the rhinoceros' back would slope.

3.

Add ears, an eye, a smile,
and two mighty horns!

4.

Then, draw two legs - front and back one.

5.

Move on to the next two legs, the tail, and hooves. You can also erase any unnecessary lines.

6.

Finally, add a sparkle in the eye, and you're done!

85

SEAL

Baby seals literally grow before your eyes, gaining weight at a rate of up to 4.5 funts per day!

1.

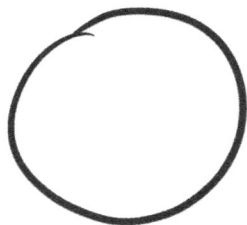

Start with a circle - this will be the head.

2.

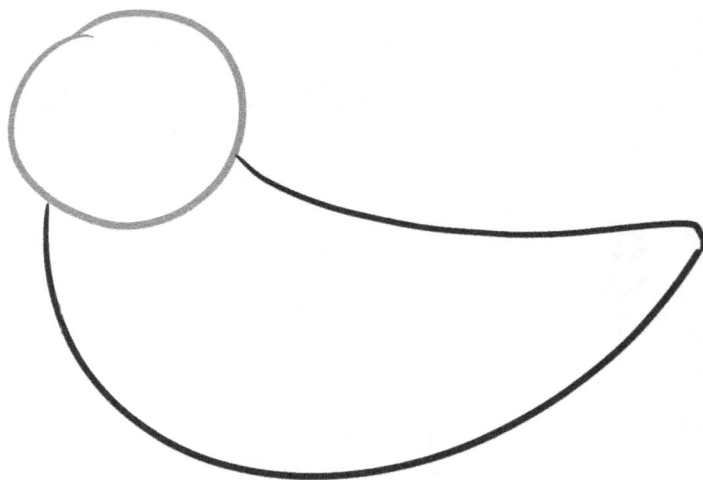

Next, draw an elongated, curved shape, resembling a banana - this will be the seal's body.

3.

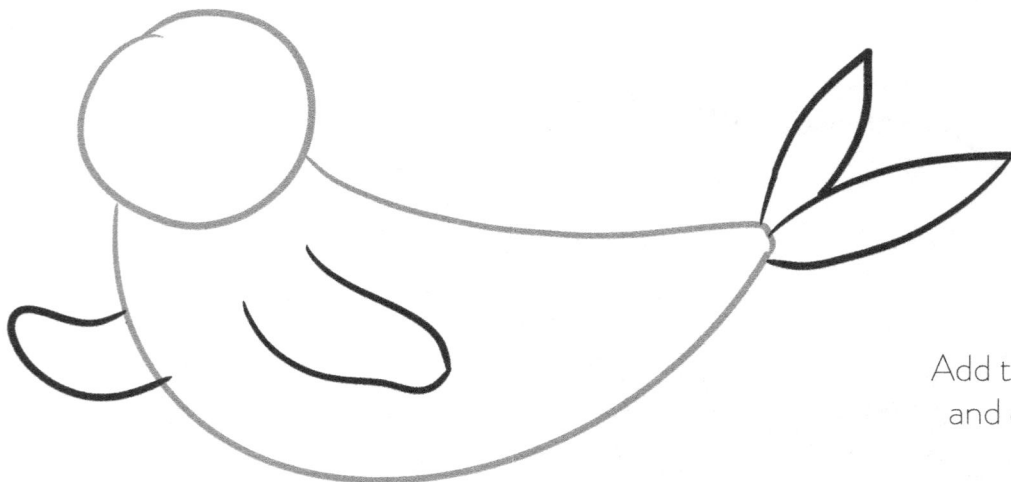

Add the front flippers and one on the tail.

4.

Include a muzzle - similar to a dog's.

5.

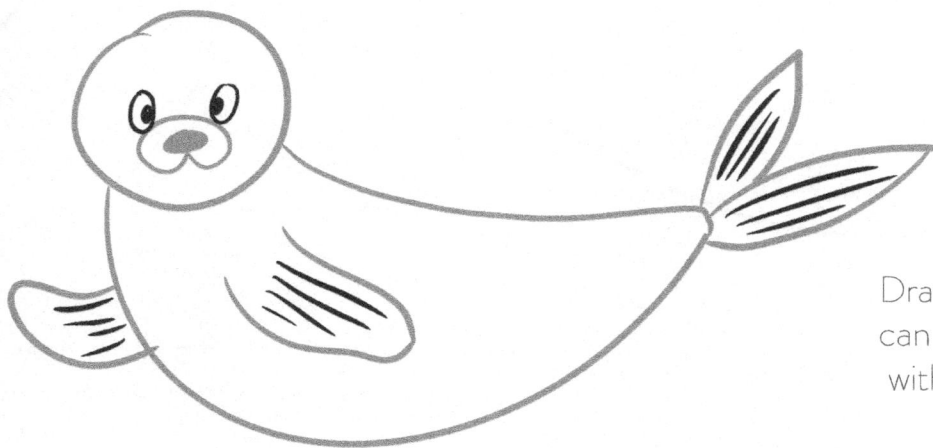

Draw the eyes and you can outline the flippers with lines along them.

6.

Finally, add some details like whiskers or eyebrows - done!

SHARK

The Whale Shark (Rhincodon typus) is like the gentle giant of the sea! It's the biggest fish around, stretching over 40 feet long and weighing more than 20 tons!

1.

Start with a gently curved arch for the shark's belly.

2.

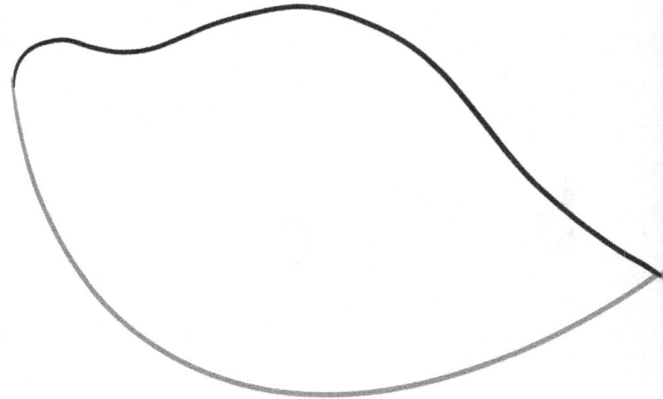

Then, closing the shark's body, draw a line on top resembling a bit of a hat shape.

3.

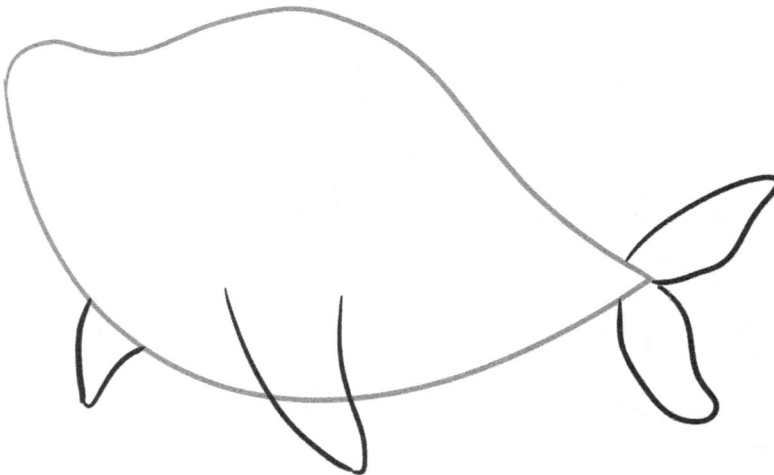

Add the front fins and the characteristic shark tail.

4.

Now, about halfway through the shark's body, draw a line gently following the arch. This is the line separating belly from the back.

5.

Add the characteristic dorsal fin, a wide smile, a big eye, and the gills - three lines below the eye.

6.

Finally, arm that wide smile with a row of sharp teeth, and we've got a shark!

89

SHEEP

Sheep can remember the faces of up to 50 other sheep for as long as 2 years!

1.

Start with a fluffy, elongated oval shape - this will be the sheep's mane.

2.

Then draw a circle below - this will be the head.

3.

Draw another fluffy oval shape - this will be the body.

4.

From the mane, draw the ears.

5.

Add eyes and a wide smile.

6.

Finally, draw four legs, and use curved lines to emphasize the fluffy texture of the sheep.

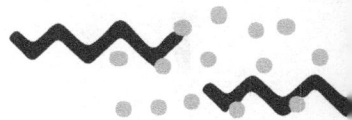

SNAIL

Did you know that snails are eye experts? They can actually regrow their eyes if they lose them!

1.

Start with a spiral shape.

2.

Continue the spiral.

3.

Close the snail's shell with a gentle curve.

4.

Draw protruding eyes within a short distance from the shell.

5.

Sketch the snail's body – feel free to experiment with different shapes here.

6.

Finally, add pupils to the eyes, a smile, and draw curved lines at the bottom of the snail's body to emphasize its folds.

SNAKE

Snakes smell with their flickering tongues!

1.

Draw a circle - that's the head.

2.

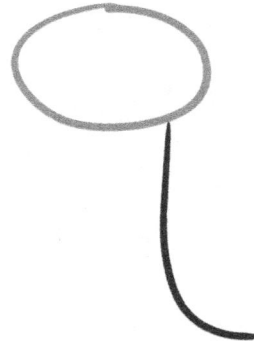

Draw a line shaped like the letter L.

3.

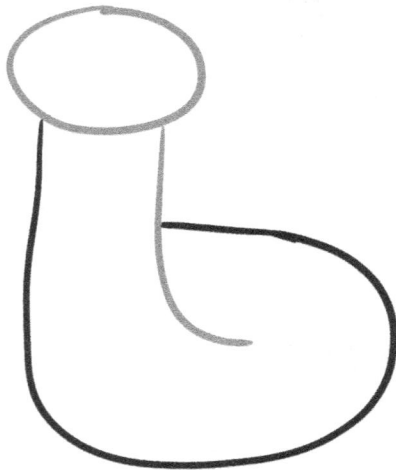

Now, on the other side of the head, draw
an arc connected to the previous line.

4.

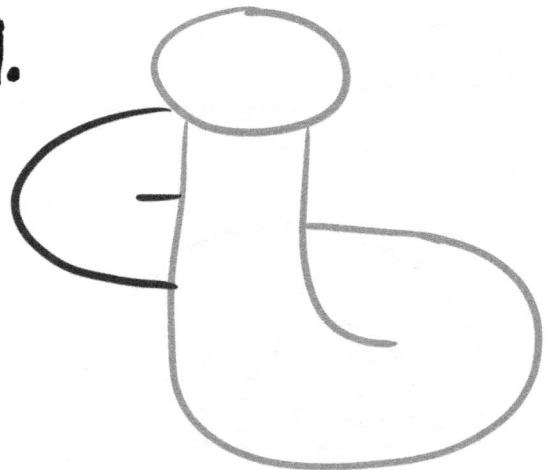

Continue drawing the snake's body
using a C-shaped line.

5.

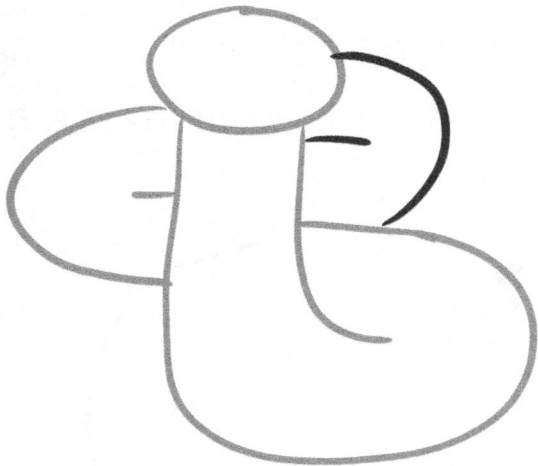

Do the same on the other side.

6.

Add the end of the tail, and you've got the whole snake.

7.

Add eyes, a nose, and a long, flickering tongue.

8.

Finally, you can decorate the snake however you like, maybe with spots!

 # SQUiRREL

Squirrels are super jumpers. They can leap up to 10 times higher than their own body length. They can also freeze on a tree at any moment during climbing.

1.

Draw a circle - that's the head.

2.

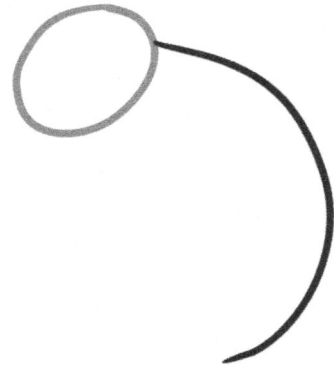

Draw a curved line - this is the squirrel's back

3.

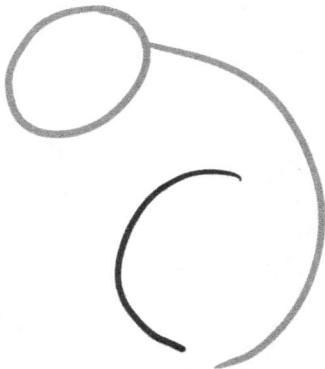

Draw a smaller C-shaped curve - that's the thigh.

4.

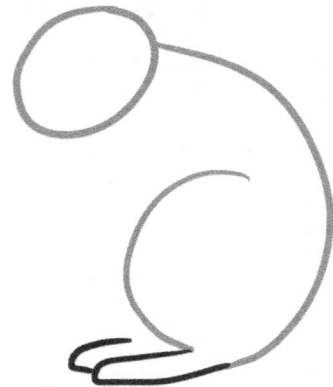

Add two legs.

5.

Draw the belly and front paws.

6.

Use two parallel S-shaped
lines to draw the squirrel's tail.

7.

Add eyes, ears with tufts,
a nose, whiskers, and a smile.

8.

Finish with additional details
as you like. Done!

TIGER

There are no two identical tigers because of their stripes, which decorate their fur and skin, they are unique to each tiger - just like fingerprints for humans.

1.

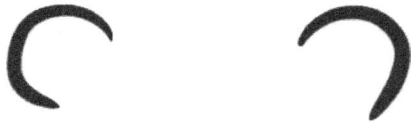

Start with two round ears.

2.

Then draw the shape of the head.

3.

Inside the head, draw
a circle for the muzzle.

4.

Add the nose, eyes, and smile.

5.

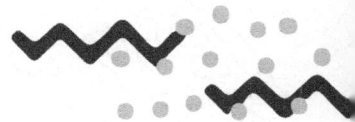

Insert an arched line for the back
and a line for the front leg.

6.

Draw four legs and a belly.

7.

Add a tail.

8.

Finally, claws and most importantly -
dark stripes all over the tiger's body!

TURTLE

The gender of a turtle can be identified by the characteristic sounds they make. Males chirp, while females hiss.

1.

Start with the shape of the top part of the shell.

2.

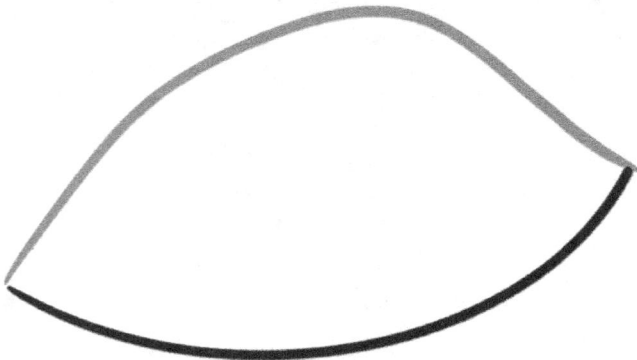

Then, close the shell with a gentle curve from the bottom.

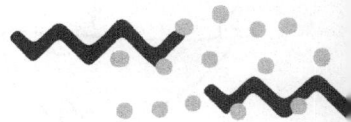

3.

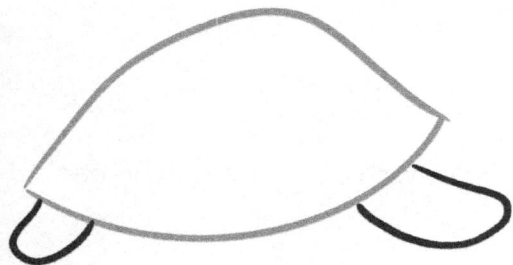

Draw the legs - front
and back.

4.

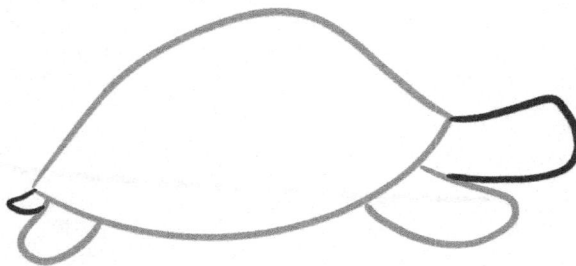

Add the head and tail.

5.

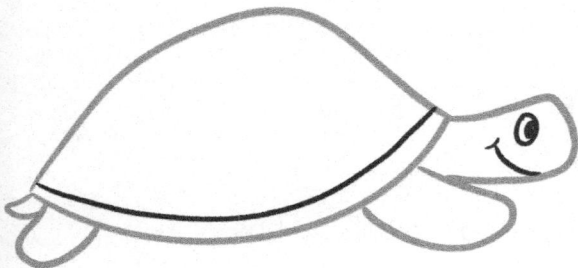

Draw an eye, a smile, and a line
at the bottom of the shell.

6.

Add claws and spots
on the shell, done!

WHALE

The heart of a whale can beat only about 9 times per minute, while the human heart beats about 90 times per minute.

1. Start with a flat line for the back.

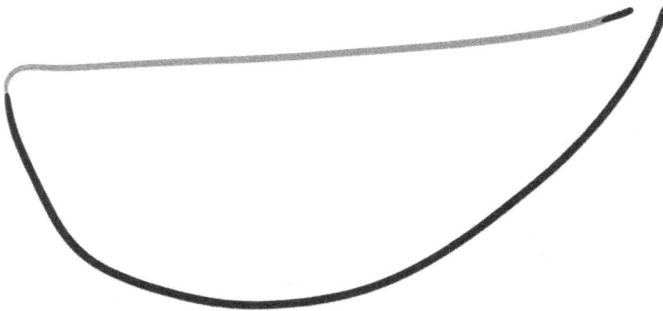

2. Draw a curved line closing the lower part of the whale's body.

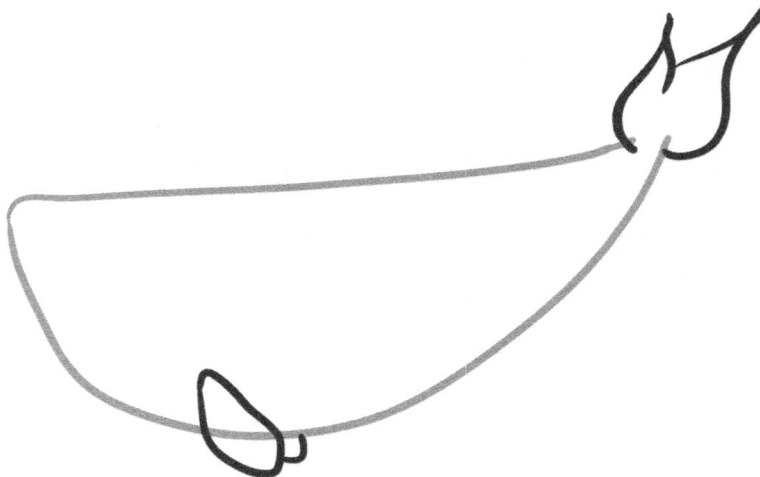

3. Add the tail and fins.

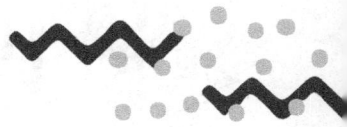

4.

Insert an eye and a smile.
Erase unnecessary lines.

5.

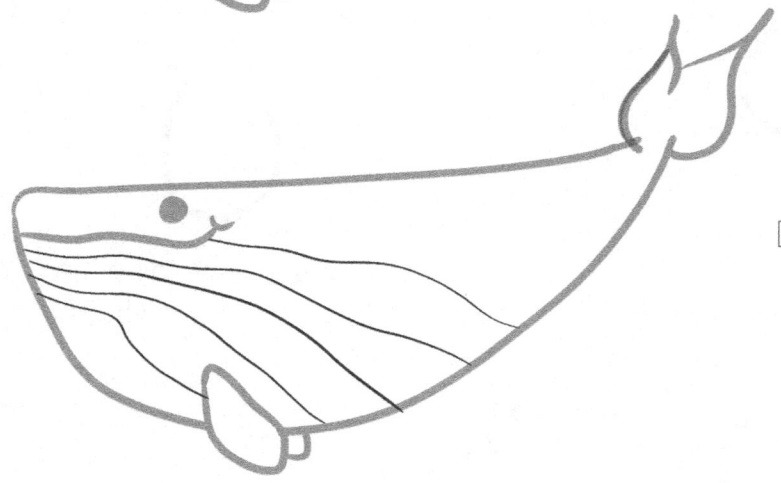

Draw lines on the belly.

6.

Add color and splashing
water from the blowhole.

WOLF

Wolves can perform long jumps, which is useful for hunting. They can leap over obstacles as high as 8 feet.

1.

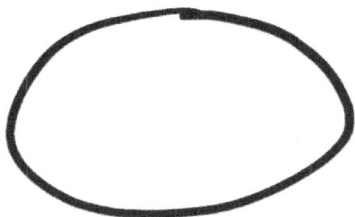

Start with a gently flattened oval shape - this will be the wolf's head.

2.

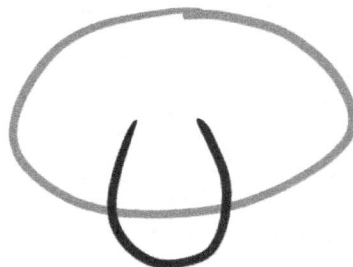

Draw a U-shape extending beyond the oval of the head - this will be the muzzle.

3.

Add pointy, large ears.

4.

Draw eyes, and on the muzzle, at the center of the bottom headline, draw a black nose, below it a mouth, and wolf fangs.

5. Add an oval for the body.

6. Then draw all four paws, whiskers, and refine the ears.

7. Add a big, fluffy tail.

8. Finish with details as desired -
like claws, cheek stripes, etc.

ZEBRA

Each zebra has unique patterns on its fur,
much like humans have different fingerprints.

1.

Start with drawing a tilted U shape
- this will be the zebra's head.

2.

Draw a gentle curve at the bottom of our
shape - this will be the muzzle. Add ears.

3.

Draw an eye, nostril, and a smile.

4.

Add a curved line to outline the back
of the head, the back arch,
a prominent rump, and a hind leg.

5.

Add a round belly.

6.

Draw four legs.

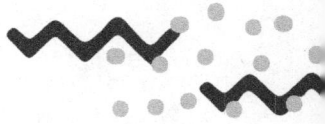

7.

Close the legs with hooves,
add a mane and a tail.

8.

Finally, what's most important
for a zebra - the black stripes!

THANK YOU!

Dear parents, when creating this "How to Draw..." book series, our goal was to offer a tool that helps your children draw with ease, beginning from the most basic shapes. We believe that this approach will bring children immense joy as they watch adorable animals come to life from simple circles, ovals and lines. If you find this book beneficial, please share your feedback, which could help others in making their choice. We wish you and your child many delightful moments of creativity and fun!

Made in the USA
Monee, IL
09 June 2024